Library of—

Library of—

Dan Beachy-Quick

TE
Textshop Editions

Clinton, MA ❦ Redondo Beach, CA
2021

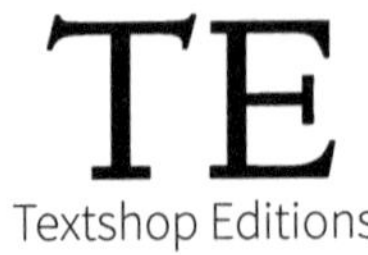

Textshop Editions is a collaborative project dedicated to producing this limited series of experimental writing.
It was founded by
K. A. Wisniewski & Piotr Florczyk.
More information may be found at
http://TextshopExperiments.org/TextshopEditions

Cataloging-in-Publication Data is available
at the Library of Congress

Library of Congress Control Number:
2021951339

First printing, December 2021

Book Design by K. A. Wisniewski

ISBN-13:
978-1-7364658-2-0

Printed in the United States of America

CONTENTS

Library Of– / 7

Afterword / 45

Acknowledgments / 51

Biography / 52

Library Of—

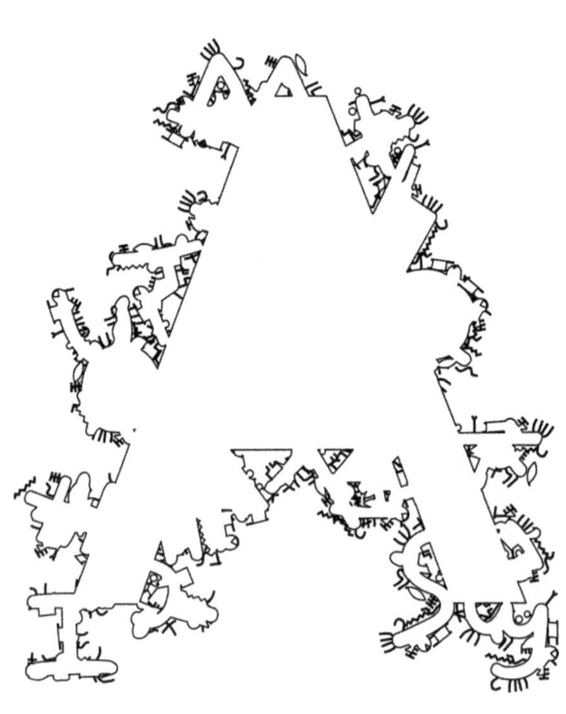

A.

.

. .

. . .

at

oms. el

lips

es.

. . .

. .

.

B.

Of broken shells—. & the sea—.
There's a book I want to read

but I don't know how. To read—.
Venus shines small light on dark loam.

The black-headed gulls—.The wind—.
The waves break open another

page that's not a page. Nothing
here says I alone.

Sea-spray—. I heard someone
say the body came of—. The foam—.

C.

Of crow logic—

faith floods the world
& the fool holds on—

a plank across a synapse
a board above abyss—.

Make a nest in virtue—
so dearly the dove

with no grammar does—
empty mouth or olive—

where home is—is

the conditional mood—

regret flies over the ocean
back, hope flies

over across the sea—
would says the dove—

could or *couldn't* says the crow.

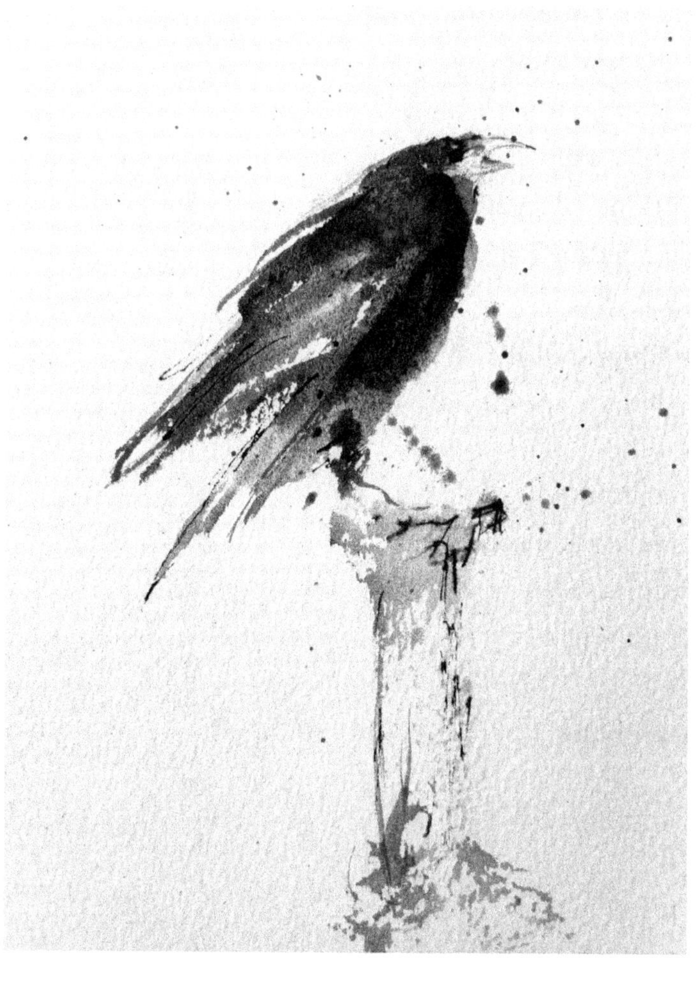

D.

Desire is the space between
stars. Distance is
the space within

an apple, a bird, a brain.
A dream of daughters in heaven
diagramming sentences:

The moon is bright. It’s not
a light.

Child bent over
a page, erasing nouns and
adjectives, all
that isn’t right:

The is not a.

E.

Eider duck winter sleep
on the froze open sea

these syllables carry care
this blood stays warm as spring

this mind wants to wake
inside what it builds
a nest there on the stones made
of winter's breast-plucked down

F.

Forget me not
is whose command to give
the feeling of awe got over me
watching my child lace her shoe
the dog opened his mouth
and in the bee flew

the hard work isn't some agony—

the mouth opens the grass grows
its tangle in the mind those loose strands
memory pulls the knot tighter
her hair as she runs by a band poorly bound

G.

Of glacial water melted in glass tubes—.
Columns not classical—. Not
holding high the roof beams—.
Of those gods—. Light
bends down—.

Apollo's temple at Delphi
the ruins in memory
the genitive of separation
what from what leaves
the columns fell almost all
the walls know you
don't know yourself so much
remains excessive in the
mind the letter hovering alone
invisible in the air

E

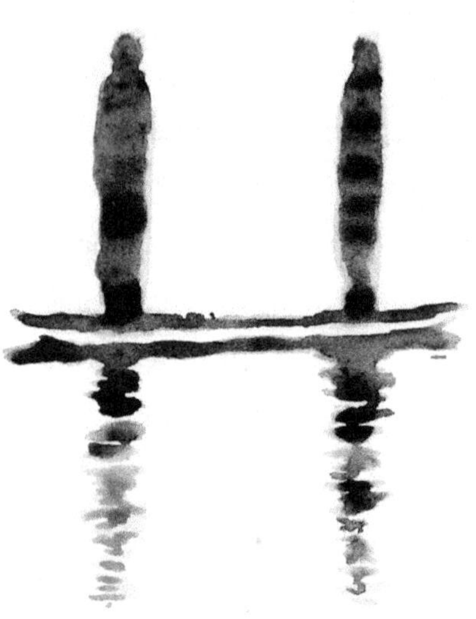

H.

Of the hero inside death
who has words has a first principle
to sing until the song doesn't exist

moisture in the soil and the seed
who says the earth floats
a piece of wood on water

an oath sworn on the river Styx
hero who thought stone
drawing iron near

had a soul and thought all
things were full of gods hero who
looking up at a star fell down in a hole

I.

And the one called Iris is also a cloud,
purple, and yellow, and red to the sight—
and the one called Hana is also a sun,
and the sun is ignited clouds—.
                                        And the I-it
that is an altar a child made; a column;
a caryatid walking with a fragment
of the temple roof on her head,
offering to others this weight of the sky;
block-tower; girder in the rubble; stalk
of winter wheat; stubble-field
of September corn—.
                                        And the more humble
forms, the lower-case, below us, yet ourselves;
the tree a child draws, green circle on a pencil-
thin line; and dandelion gone to seed—.
                                                            And
the one that makes his wish—.
To have no idea—.

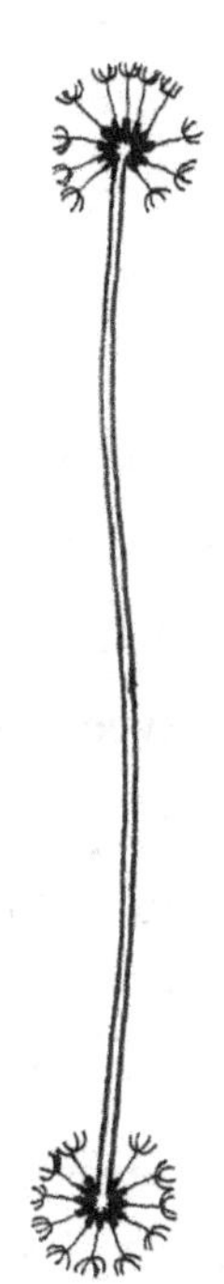

J.

Of Justice who covers her breasts,
turns aside in the kitchen to turn
the radio on. Threatens with furies
the sun if it loosens its measure.
Scents fire with spices and breathes in
The flame. Says the soul speaks
the language of ears and eyes. Says
war is what is shared. Says war is
president of all. Says salt-water gives life
to fish but kills a man. Says a donkey
lusts after trash. Not gold. Weeping
sweeps the kitchen floor. Says
as child is to father, man is to—. Who
will not say the next word. What is
born from fire, to fire returns. All is.
Even night. Even the child's eyes—
even the child she teaches to breathe
under water. Swimming lessons. The principle
that tunes the lyre—. Tunes the bow—.

K.

Of kings and queens

nightly

they fill

their chamberpots—.

. . . memories of sentences read years ago:
Montaigne's "On Experience" . . .

Thinking truth is not a
world or word apart from this world
the pain of the kidney stone
in the penis must also be included

in the Royal Laws

L.

Of the lost child, child
who feels her heart's gone missing,
child who wanders from fear far
into the woods, who

makes of leaves a crown to cover
her head, child who chases
the creatures that run from her rule—
white-eye of rabbit's tail, green

disc glowing of the deer's midnight eye—
who puzzles out the path
where thought alone makes the nettles tremble
and walks it, child who

enters a cave, finds the night
is rooted there, and in the husk the sun
dropped as it rose, she makes her bed,
that child, that seed.

M.

My   my
memory my   my mind
the theory   thinks it thinks
my mansion my   home
memory and those   rooms of
closed doors   crumbling walls

for a long time   silence astonished
my heart   my memory cloud
a complex song   eyes
and thunderbolt and   one grain
of millet dropped makes   a sound
what is there to think is there

to think   upload   invoice
subject heading no   attachment
there's the child on a cloud   laughing
there's the child who sings along
there's the child who disappears
when the father writes down   the song

N.

Of noman—
that name is an echo in the blind monster's cave—.

What grammar keeps these ghosts at their labor?

The silent letter 'h'—. The silent letter 'g'—.

Of gnomon—
the triangle on the sundial that is the one that knows—.

You do your thinking by sunlight or torchlight—.
You make a shadow to see—. But who are you?

Noman. Gnomon. Here's my shadow—.

Tell me what day it is. What day is. What time.

O.

O limits of the nest
O hidden math of peas in pod
O holy bean field not to be crossed
O honey drone
O torn green scent on fingers
O partial knowledge
O infant tongue
O wisdom stolen from books on loan
O harmonies that make the planets chime
O sty on the child's eye
O violent artificer
O metempsychosis of vegetable soul
O purple aster
O daughter with the tangled hair
O vow of silence
O word of mouth
O torn page of sacred cares

P.

Paths deer find
their own foot formed—

can it be true—
through the thought-tangle—

all—the thinkable
arrives.

Is the burr—my theology—.
Or the thistle—.

I see the sun is
a purple bloom above the thorns—.

I study these hooks
and barbs—.

Q.

Of questions
    no inventiveness
        can find—

        I think
    I'm not thinking
yet. It is

done to me
    what I think
        I do myself.

            Point my finger
    in the passive
tense. Or is it

a mood—. The
    the passive mood—.
        Where is what was

            so near. Deerness—.
    Other thoughts
that leap in fear away

from thinking.
Is it fear—.
Or a field—.

Grass inside a
question. No
idea is as green.

R.

—of rituals of purification, of the root-bearing fields,
of the right hand as a leaf held up to the sun,
or resonance, of desire, of roman rings found
in urns shattered by the plow, of raccoons
stealing minnows from the bait can in moonlight,
of rest and restless dreams, of her robe's loose knot,
of love and strife and restoring back to life
a woman who stopped breathing, of a voice
calling a name through the air, of a philosopher
walking to the volcano's edge and jumping in,
of theories of return, of resurrection, of recognition
of being or becoming a god, of ash, of recorded memory,
of a bronze sandal found after the mountain erupts,
of repeated lessons in old books, of the child
who calls herself goddess of rainbows, of the child
reading song lyrics on her glowing screen,
of relative motion, of memory in the recursive mind,
of seed-sown rows, of seeds planted in the runnels
of the ears, of conference registrations, of rectitude,
of religious mystics and their beds of stinging nettles,
of rent overdue, of realization, of harmony as glue—

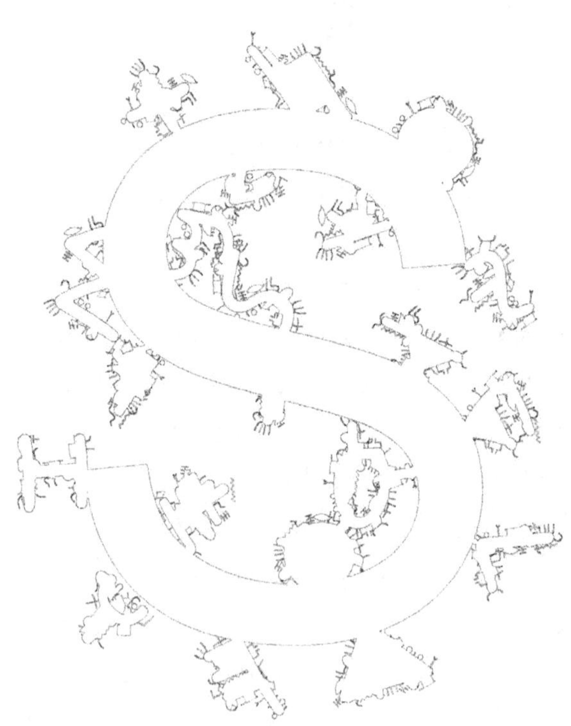

S.

Sun and counter-sun
is what is sayable what is
said or unsaid or do vaster
entanglements wreck the sum
of love and strife and
that fire around which
the human eye gathers
the adequate idea is
angles with no passion
God's own geometry
a lantern behind veils
keeps its flame a flame
the subconscious flicker
the lit wick stays blind
in wind and/or at night

T.

Of time
the ancient scholars agree
it created itself
it was not
created

it makes personal the condition
life calls itself life

but we say time
in secret to ourselves

U.

un-

negates

um-

pauses

*

I wanted to think about the universe.
How it came to be.
How in it there are rabbits, stars, memories, children.
I wanted to think about others thinking
how thought is the blood around the human heart.
I found in myself old fears; only some of them were mine.
What is thought about turns away from thinking.
What is spoken about turns away from words.
I wanted to find the proper invocation.
Not the goddess to sing wrath; not the god to sing power.
Word that opens within itself an honest void.
A mind-nest; a house of brooding.

*

unum
unum

V.

Of atoms in the void
where the monads assemble memory—
you beetle dark as the wild carrot's dark petal
you pythagorean theorem you proof on a page
you principle running naked down the hall you wife
you child wandering the dunes
the cask can hold the wine but also the winseskins the wine was in
and so of the child's first philosophy
putting her head in the water letting breath escape her lips
the bubbles that rise through the element
demonstrate the quiet work of that god named fear
who sets in motion those atoms that would not move
rising from heart to mind a face inside each or is that love
the god named love or the god named thought
I thought a little knowledge would help me
as wings help sparrows I thought open books could fly
but I'm not a child I don't get out of the water and cry

W.

Of the letter *w*
who sometimes on silent wings

wren
write

nests in the eye but not in the ear

holy homonym
and sacred ritual

of how to disappear in plain sight

X.

Let X equal a man.
For many years, X has dreamed of tornadoes—
  first in fear, then of wanting the wind to hit him.
Once X dreamed lightning struck
  his right hand, but he woke to no scar.
Twice in his life X dreamed about heaven—
  first, not knowing how he'd died, he walked
  into a green field where others wandered,
  some of whom he recognized; he met his wife
  in that meadow; she was still alive.
  In the next dream heaven was a mountain lodge
  with dark wainscoting, and one of the guests
  warned X that it can get so boring that you can lose
  your mind, pointing out a man
  who stared at a small refrigerator.
X dreamed he was a dolphin swimming under a river
  covered by ice, and his wife was a hawk flying above him.
X dreamed a child and the child came true—
  the child fell asleep and dreamed about a cricket
  in the desert.
Let Y equal the child.
For X some books he's read stay in him as do dreams
  uncertainly remembered things:

Like the page that spoke of one's life being a sentence
    an invisible pencil writes at night—
    and the sentence that the sun is an eternal fire within us.
X had another child—it's true.
She's real, X tells himself.
X knows there's a problem to solve; for a long time
    he desired to solve it himself, but he couldn't
    learn how to think.
Now X knows he's part of the problem.
In the dream he hasn't yet had, the moon is his
    teacher, and she writes in chalk
    on the blackboard night, *Solve for X*.

Y.

Why? asks the child—
I agree, but the answer's wrong.
Later she says: *Yesterday is yellow.*
Eating the sun-yolk of an egg.
Trying to remember the question.

*

Why me? asks the child
    hardly a child anymore.

My lyric register needs some repair.
You, I say, I want to say, you—

but the pronoun grows vague.

Z.

Of zero—

the air within it thinks
as the hot air inside the sun also thinks—

it is great, powerful, eternal,
immortal and possessed
of wide knowledge—

it creates a bound around all
within it, marking love's outermost limit,
erasing itself by establishing
the innermost distance—

final sum the numbers reach—
even the numbers, those gods—

Of Zeno—

Sitting on a stone
behind my eye, teaching me
my prayers:

Let Achilles lose the stadium footrace—.

Let the shot arrow be still in the air—.

AFTERWORD

I struggle with eternity, but don't we all? When John Keats wrote in a letter that he wants to become one of the immortal poets I cannot help but think of the tense of the verb—a letter he wrote, and is not still writing. Even in grammar there is a little mortal fate. When in "Ode to a Nightingale" I read

> Thou wast not born for death, immortal Bird!
>   No hungry generations tread thee down;
> The voice I hear this passing night was heard
>   In ancient days by emperor and clown:
> Perhaps the self-same song that found a path
>   Through the sad heart of Ruth, when, sick for home,
>   She stood in tears amid the alien corn…

some kind of deathlessness in spite of death becomes a little clearer. The song lives forever as itself, the same liquid notes, in the mortal casement of countless thrushes. A little god in the voicebox whose eternity hides within until the song unfolds it into the world. But a poem's eternity feels different. For example, no one sings exactly the same song.

If I could sit down to write—at a tavern with a flower garden, or underneath a plum tree—and compose myself the very poem that Keats himself wrote, then the condition

I suffer would be the thrush-condition; and you, you'd suffer just the same, person-poet-bird, and could write the same poem again I just wrote again, and so—sad Ruth, sad emperor, sad clown—could you. But it isn't so—or, at least, it hasn't shown me it is so yet. Though sometimes I also feel a drowsy numbness gather like thick-honey around my senses.

Then I think of other eternities. I think of Pythagoras who, walking down the street of ancient Athens heard a dog bark, bent down and embraced the stray, hearing in the cur's yelp the voice of an old friend. Pythagoras lived many lives, so he said, and remembered each one of them: once he was Euphorbus, and once Aethalides. Then his soul wandered into and out of plants and animals, wandered through the underworld. He became Hermotimus, Pyrrhus, and when Pyrrhus died—that fisherman who lived on the holy island of Delos—he became Pythagoras. But that's not the eternity I'm singing either, that single golden thread of conscious experience never shorn apart. It is the *tetractys*, spiritual core of the Pythagorean cult, marker of musical harmonies and the seasons, marker of the holy ratios, that is on my mind:

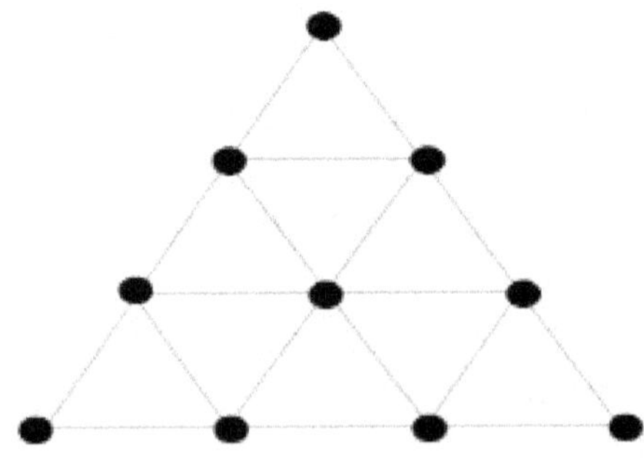

No initiate into the mysteries myself, I have nonetheless pondered these points. I began to sense something that shook the thick honey out of my mind. That these points, this shape, this *dekad*, are themselves not just an image of what one might call a god, but are gods themselves. They are eternal, but can be so only by any given mortal life grasping that impossible fact, learning the harmonies, reciting the ratios. I felt to me as if the human mind exists so that the *tetractys* may also; that the web of neurons wove itself around this immortal idea that can be in the world in no other way than by the thinking it made possible. It made itself possible; it did so through us.

But of musical harmonies and sacred math I know profanely little. But the thought lodged in my head, a minor god. A little daemon. A modest genius.

Visiting Iceland some years later to offer a paper on lyric consciousness, I visited Roni Horn's permanent art installation, *Library of Water*. In a former local library, Horn installed twenty-four clear cylinders each filled with the melted water of one of Iceland's famed—and receding—glaciers. The world seen through the water bends along the curve of the glass, making sight aware of itself, adding to the mundane daily seen through any window an uncanny sense of impermanence, of being somehow more than, and less than, real. An archive of vital element, the *Library of Water* evokes consciousness even as it prods conscience. Perhaps that is as it must be. To learn to think and feel a necessary guilt there in the mind as its fundamental ground. Perhaps that is how we learn to care. Water is our own life's primary constituent element. Those melting glaciers signal loss of unimaginable scope. Both cities underwater, and thirst's drought. Worse, if worse there can be, this uncanny understanding: that we have betrayed the element we bear inside us.

Eternity bears a wound. I suppose Pythagoras knew it all along.

But it is from that wounded sense of timelessness—a wound maybe it is truest to call time—that *Library Of—* arrived. Keats's nightingale, Pythagoras's *tetractys*, and Roni Horn's cylinders of glacial melt, brought my thinking to the alphabet, those twenty-six letters whose illimitable permutations create the words we write and speak. I thought of each letter not as syllable, sign, or phoneme, but as a vessel of a kind. I thought of each letter as I learned to think of the ten points of the *tetractys*, minor gods enwrapped in the larger harmony of the whole to which each is vital, contributing part. I thought this small pantheon—*a b c d e f g h i j k l m n o p q r s t u v w x y z*—built a temple around it called a living mind, and made the strange threshold of the senses for windows and doors so the world could sneak in, ask us to think, and offer a little pang of guilt to pain the heart. Each letter I imagined as an archive itself, filled almost completely with a catalog of memory and experience, speculation and rumor, bankrupt belief and shining fact; and that, just as the glaciers are receding, so the archive of every letter slips into oblivion as our carelessness wears away the world.

I wanted each poem here to remember what otherwise will be forgotten, little portions of time kept in one of eternity's forms—time growing ever more full as we run out of it, eternity ever more empty. I imagine each letter, each poem, as the crux of that irony. A tense space of memory and association. What one small life can add to vast library. A sense that my own life is just a book on loan.

ACKNOWLEDGMENTS

Abundant gratitude to Piotr Florczyk and K. A. Wisniewski of Textshop Editions, for making a standalone chapbook of *Library Of—* & the vital vision of their press. Thank you to Jeffrey Levine for advices on vision and revision. Thank you to Del Harrow, Marius Lehene, and Mai Wagner, for the art works that grace those pages.

BIOGRAPHY

Dan Beachy-Quick is a poet, essayist, and translator. His most recent books include Arrows (Tupelo 2020) and a translation of ancient Greek lyric poetry, Stone-Garland (Milkweed Editions 2020). His work has been supported by the Monfort, Lannan, and Guggenheim Foundations. He teaches at Colorado State University, where he is an University Distinguished Teaching Scholar.

OTHER TITLES BY TEXTSHOP EDITIONS

Defense Mechanism by Krzysztof Siwczyk

Sonnet 100 by Marilyn Allen

www.ingramcontent.com/pod-product-compliance
Lightning Source LLC
LaVergne TN
LVHW010545100826
845148LV00013B/2605

* 9 7 8 1 7 3 6 4 6 5 8 2 0 *